A Romantic Sketchbook for Piano

BOOK II

37 moderately easy pieces composed *c*. 1825 – *c*. 1950

Selected and edited by Alan Jones

The pieces in this album, of about Grades 3–4 in standard, have been selected to provide a variety of keys, time signatures, tempi, styles and moods.

Original source material has been followed, but obvious errors and minor inconsistencies in phrasing and dynamics have been corrected without specific comment. New fingering has been added, and the signs ⌞ and ⌜ are used to indicate the right hand and left hand respectively. Editorial suggestions for pedalling and for metronome marks are shown within square brackets but should not be considered in any way authoritative. Other editorial matters are mentioned in the footnotes to the pieces.

The titles to the pieces are given in English, either original or in translation, with the foreign-language titles in brackets beneath.

Alan Jones

The Associated Board of
the Royal Schools of Music

Contents

III B 6

III B 4

➡✳⬅

STUDY in A minor

MAYER, Op.340 No.2

Born in Prussia to a clarinettist father and a piano teacher mother, Charles Mayer (1799–1862) was taken as a baby with his family to Russia, where he later studied the piano with Field. He taught in St Petersburg for 30 years, as well as touring throughout Europe giving piano recitals, and then settled in Dresden for the last decade of his life. He composed a vast number of piano works, mainly for teaching purposes.

WALTZ in A flat

SCHUBERT, D.365/3

In his short working life, the Viennese-born Franz Schubert (1797–1828) produced a remarkable output of music of different genres. Although essentially a Classical composer in his symphonic works, his poetic sensibility, particularly in the development of the solo song as a special art form, looks ahead to the early Romantic era. Among his many piano works he wrote over 400 dances, many of them improvised at social evenings among friends. In this waltz, the dynamics and pedalling are editorial.

STUDY in A

LEMOINE, Op.37 No.40

Henry Lemoine (1786–1854) was born in Paris and studied at the Conservatoire. He became a well-known teacher of the piano and wrote a methodical tutor for the instrument, as well as many educational compositions which are more than mere pedagogic studies. On his father's death in 1817, he took over the management of the family music publishing business and ran it successfully until his own death, during which time he published most of Chopin's music.

D.C. a tempo al Fine

THE CLEAR STREAM
(Le courant limpide)

J. F. BURGMÜLLER, Op.100 No.7

Born in Bavaria, Johann Friedrich Burgmüller (1806–1874) belonged to a musical family, his younger brother Norbert being a gifted composer who died at an early age. As a young man, Friedrich settled in Paris where he became a popular pianist, improvising hundreds of salon pieces and composing many works for the amateur player. Today he is only remembered by teachers and students for his Op.100 & 109 studies. In this one, the pedalling is editorial and the composer's somewhat fast MM (♩ = 176) has been revised.

STUDY in C minor

Andante quasi allegretto [♩ = c.100]

con espressione

HELLER, Op.125 No.16

Born in Hungary near Pest, Stephen Heller (1813–1888) was a child prodigy pianist and toured Europe until he suffered a nervous breakdown. In due course he settled in Paris, where he tried to earn a living as a pianist, critic and composer; but, although befriended by Berlioz, Chopin and Liszt, his life was largely one of loneliness and poverty. All trace of his larger-scale works has been lost, but his short, imaginative piano pieces continue to remain popular today.

AB 2345

REAPER'S SONG

(Schnitterliedchen)

SCHUMANN, Op.68 No.18

Nicht sehr schnell [Allegretto, ♩.= c.80]

One of the foremost German composers of the Romantic era, Robert Schumann (1810–1856) was born at Zwickau in Saxony. His considerable output includes four symphonies, three concertos, about 100 choral works, chamber music, over 300 songs and much piano music. This piece comes from his *Album for the Young*, which he composed in Dresden in 1848 with his young family around him. The pedalling is taken from Clara Schumann's posthumous instructive edition, but her MM (♩.= 126) seems rather fast.

CHRISTMAS BELLS

(Jule-Klokkerne)

GADE, Op. 36 No. 1

The leading Danish composer of the 19th century, Niels Gade (1817–1890) was born in Copenhagen. Besides being a notable violinist and an orchestral conductor, he was the first head of the Royal Danish Music Conservatory. Both influenced by and admired by Mendelssohn and Schumann, he wrote eight symphonies, some choral works and much chamber and instrumental music. In this piece from his *Children's Christmas* album, the original bar-length pedalling in bb. 5–8 etc. has been modified.

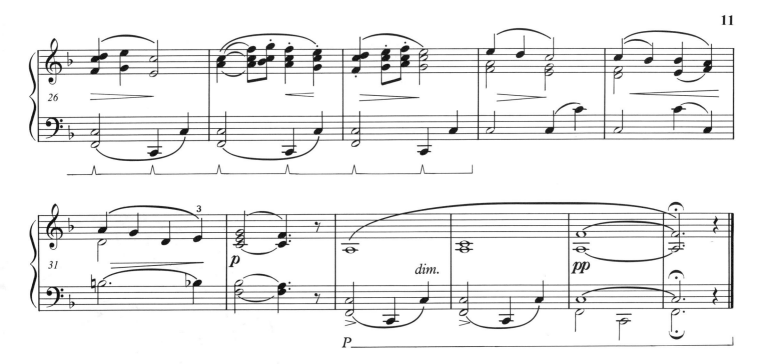

MINIATURE

T. F. KIRCHNER, Op.62 No.8

Ruhig, ausdrucksvoll [Tranquil and expressive, ♪ = c.120]

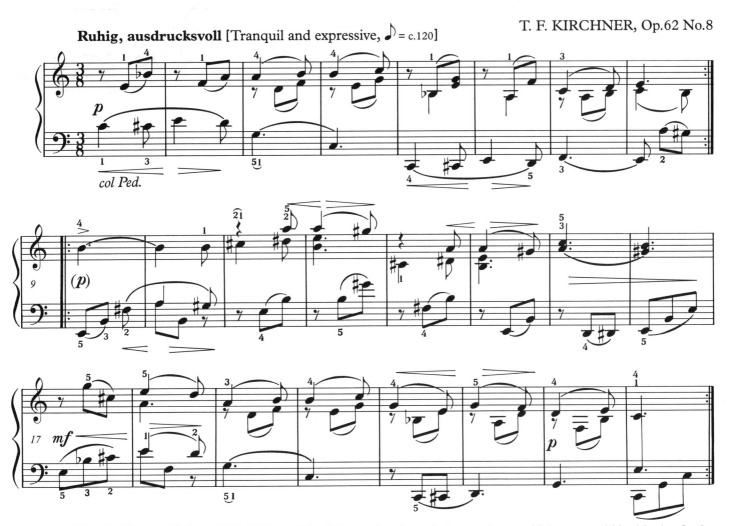

Born near Chemnitz, Theodor Kirchner (1823–1903) studied in Leipzig, where he made the acquaintance of Schumann and Mendelssohn. On the latter's recommendation, he obtained the post of organist at Winterthur in Switzerland and remained there for 20 years before moving to Zurich, where he was active as a conductor. Subsequently he taught in Würzburg, Leipzig, Dresden and Hamburg. He composed many short piano pieces in the manner of Schumann and characterised by inventive and distinctive touches.

THE CLOCK ON THE WALL

(Die Wanduhr)

Allegro vivace [♩ = c.152]

KULLAK, Op.62 No. 2

Fine

D.S. % al Fine

Born in the district of Posen (Poznán), Theodor Kullak (1818–1882) went to Berlin to study medicine but later became a piano pupil of Czerny in Vienna. In 1846 he was appointed court pianist in Berlin, where he founded a music academy which soon developed a considerable reputation throughout Europe. His compositions consist of transcriptions and arrangements for the piano as well as many teaching pieces. In this one from a children's album, an easier ossia is suggested for the l.h. in bb.9–12.

AB 2345

STUDY in F

Andante cantabile [♩ = c.104]

LOESCHHORN, Op.65 No.25

Albert Loeschhorn (1819–1905) was born in Berlin and studied at the city's Royal Institute for Church Music. He later taught the piano there, being given the title of Royal Professor, and was highly regarded as a teacher by many talented pupils. He also organised and took part in regular chamber music concerts. Although he composed many works, he is known today only for the instructive studies he wrote for the piano. The dynamics in this one are editorial.

AB 2345

LITTLE FLOWER
(Kleine Blume)

GURLITT, Op.205 No.1

Born into an artistic family in Altona when it was part of Denmark, Cornelius Gurlitt (1820–1901), a pupil of Reinecke's father, began his career as organist at the city's Cathedral. He later taught in Copenhagen and then became a professor at the Hamburg Conservatory. Greatly influenced by Schumann, he composed a variety of works but today is only known for an immense number of piano pieces, written largely for educational purposes. In an Augener edition of *Little Flowers*, this piece is entitled 'Wild Mignonette'.

AB 2345

LITTLE PIECE in E flat

FRANCK

Born in Liège of Flemish descent, César Franck (1822–1890) spent most of his life in Paris, where he became a distinguished church organist and professor of organ at the Conservatoire. Best known as a composer of orchestral and chamber music, towards the end of his life he wrote a collection of short pieces for the harmonium, intended for use by church organists and published posthumously. As this piece shows, they are equally well suited to the piano, but some editorial pedalling is suggested.

SCHERZO

REINECKE, Op.183 No.5/3

A friend of Gurlitt, also born in Altona, Carl Reinecke (1824–1910) was a proficient player of the violin and the piano, and first played in public at the age of 11. In 1844 he was appointed court pianist in Copenhagen and made a number of concert tours, performing REIN London on several occasions. Later, for 35 years he was conductor of the Gewandhaus in Leipzig, where he was also professor of composition at the Conservatory. A prolific composer, he wrote mainly for the piano, most of his output being of an instructional nature.

CRADLE SONG
(Bådnlåt)

GRIEG, Op.66 No.7

Norway's most important Romantic composer, Edvard Grieg (1843–1907) was born in Bergen (of Scottish extraction on his father's side) and studied in Leipzig and with Gade in Copenhagen. His works were inspired by the musical language of his country, as is evident in his orchestral works and more particularly in his many songs and piano pieces. A great influence was L.M. Lindeman's historic collection of Norwegian folk melodies, some of which he arranged for piano in Op.66. In this piece, the slurs are editorial.

AB 2345

WALTZ in E

BRAHMS, Op.39 No.5

One of the greatest symphonists after Beethoven and a composer of choral, vocal, chamber and piano works, Johannes Brahms (1833–1897) was born and spent his early years in Hamburg. In 1865 on a visit to Vienna, where he was later to settle permanently, he completed a set of 16 waltzes for piano duet. They were later published with two arrangements for solo piano by Brahms himself: the one difficult and the other simplified for smaller hands. In this example from the latter, some touches of pedalling will help to create a graceful effect.

AB 2345

FIRST BUNCH OF FLOWERS

(Premier bouquet)

SANDRÉ

Un peu lent et très expressif, ♩ = 66

The French composer and teacher, Gustave Sandré (1843–1916) was for many years a professor at the Nancy Conservatoire. He wrote songs, chamber works and many piano pieces, some of which were regularly published as supplements to the magazine *L'Illustration*, including an album *For the little ones*, from which this piece comes.

ALLA SICILIANA

GUILMANT, Op.48 No.2

Félix Guilmant (1837–1911) became a church organist in his native town of Boulogne at the age of 15. He later moved to Paris, where he was organist of the Trinité for 30 years and where he taught at the Conservatoire. He made numerous recital tours of Europe and America, thereby establishing a considerable reputation in the musical world. He composed much music for the organ but little for the piano. In this piece from an album possibly intended for his daughter's instruction, the pedalling is editorial.

WINTER MORNING

(Le matin en hiver)

TCHAIKOVSKY, Op. 39 No. 2

The leading 19th-century Russian composer of symphonies, concertos, operas and ballets, born in the Vyatka province, Pyotr Tchaikovsky (1840–1893) suffered misfortunes in his personal life which had an influence on his music. Some months after his unhappy marriage in 1877, and having completed his 4th Symphony and the opera *Eugene Onegin*, he retired to the country and thought it would be a pleasant relaxation to write a set of piano pieces for children in the manner of Schumann. The 24 numbers in his *Album for the Young* have remained popular ever since.

ON THE LAKE

(Auf dem See)

H. HOFMANN, Op.77 No.12

Allegretto e commodo [♩. = c.84]

Born in Berlin, Heinrich Hofmann (1842–1902) sang as a boy in the Cathedral choir and later studied the piano at Kullak's Academy. After teaching and playing the piano for several years to earn a living, he devoted the rest of his life to composition, but the popularity of his orchestral works did not outlast the century. Today he is better known for his smaller-scale works for chamber groups and for the piano. In this piece from an album of *Sketches*, the pedalling is editorial.

IMPRESSION
(Dojmy)

FIBICH, Op.41 No.108

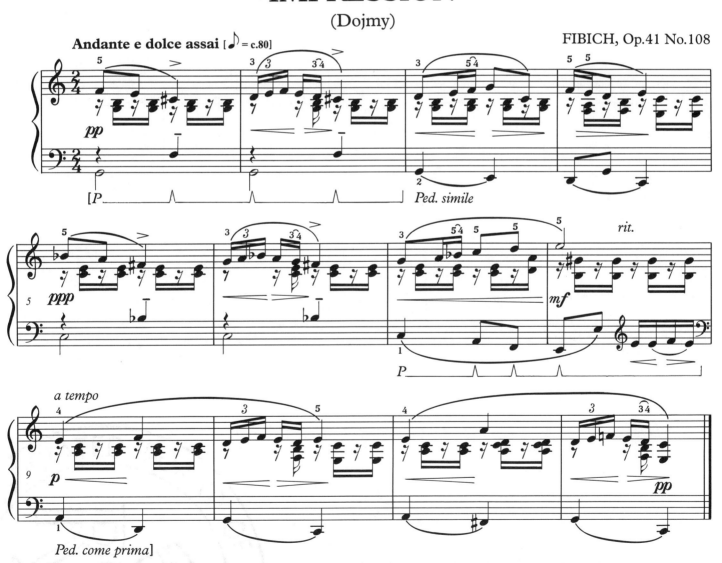

Bohemian by birth, Zdeněk Fibich (1850–1900) spent most of his life in Prague as a private teacher, conductor and choirmaster. Music for the piano formed by far the largest part of his composition output. The collection of 376 pieces entitled *Moods, Impressions and Reminiscences* was the product of his lengthy relationship with a girl pupil who later became his mistress. Whenever they met, he would present her with a new piece, the *Impressions* among other things highlighting her physical features.

SOLDIERS' MARCH

(Soldatenmarsch)

Frisch und munter [Brisk and lively, ♩ = c.116]

R. FUCHS, Op.47 No.14

Born in the Styria (Steiermark) district of Austria, Robert Fuchs (1847–1927) started to study various instruments at an early age. When he was 18, he settled in Vienna to earn a living as an organist, répétiteur and teacher. At the same time he continued his studies at the Conservatory, where he later taught a generation of musicians who included Mahler, Sibelius and Wolf. He composed orchestral, choral and chamber works as well as much piano music. This piece comes from his *Album for the Young.*

AB 2345

THE GOSSIP

(Die Schwätzerin)

P. ZILCHER, Op.55 No.4

Born in Frankfurt, Paul Zilcher (1855–1943) learned the piano with his father and taught his own son Hermann, who became a well-known teacher and composer in Germany. Besides founding the Parlow-Zilcher Piano School in Offenbach (Main), he composed a great number of piano and instrumental pieces for teaching purposes.

SEE-SAW

(Balancelle)

GODARD, Op.149 Bk 1 No.4

Benjamin Godard (1849–1895) was born in Paris and studied at the Conservatoire. A child prodigy, he had already published a number of compositions by the age of 16. He later had success with a dramatic symphony and this was followed by many works, none of which has remained in the repertory except for the Berceuse from his opera *Jocelyne*. In this piano piece from an album of *Children's Studies*, the slurs have been modified and the pedalling is editorial.

AB 2345

TYLETTE (The Cat)

ALBANESI

Carlo Albanesi (1856–1926) was born in Naples and learned the piano with his father. After touring Italy and France giving recitals, he settled permanently in England at the age of 26. Ten years later he was appointed to a professorship of piano at the Royal Academy of Music, and he also became an examiner for the Associated Board. His compositions include a few chamber works, some songs, six piano sonatas and other piano pieces. This one comes from his 'Tyltyl' Suite.

VILLAGE MERRIMENT

(Die Freude im Dorfe)

SCHÜTT, Op.105 No.5

Born in St Petersburg, Eduard Schütt (1856–1933) gave up a career in commerce to study music in his native city and in Leipzig. At the age of 22 he moved to Vienna to become conductor of the Akademischer Wagner-Verein. As a pianist he made many successful tours playing chamber music and performing his own concertos. Among his other compositions are numerous songs and many poetic miniatures for piano.

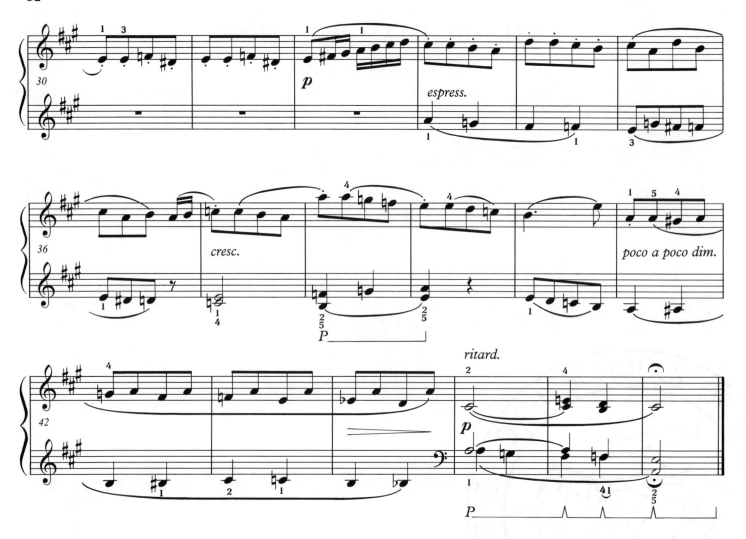

A PUZZLE
(Gorelky – ein Geduldspiel)

KARGANOV, Op.25 No.2

Génari Karganov (1858–1890) was born in Georgia and studied under Reinecke at the Leipzig Conservatory. In 1879 he settled in Tbilisi, where he taught and wrote music criticism, dying at the early age of 31. Strongly influenced by Tchaikovsky and Rimsky-Korsakov, he composed mainly for the piano, and most of his works were of an instructional nature. In this piece from his *Album for the Young*, the title may mean either 'A Puzzle' or 'A Game of Patience'.

THE SAILOR

SOMERVELL

Born in Windermere, Sir Arthur Somervell (1863–1937) studied composition under Stanford at Cambridge University, in Berlin and at the Royal College of Music, where later he was to teach. Although he composed a few orchestral works, his reputation today rests largely upon five song cycles. He took a great interest in music education, being a school inspector for many years, and wrote six operettas and many piano pieces for children. This one comes from an album of *Holiday Pictures*.

PASTORAL SCENE
(Ländliche Szene)

Allegretto [♩ = c.120]

REBIKOV, Op.10 No.1

Born in Siberia, Vladimir Rebikov (1866–1920) studied music in various cities. He resided for periods in Kiev, Odessa, Kishinev, Berlin, Vienna and Moscow, and died at Yalta. He was a noted writer on music, particularly on opera of which he himself composed ten works, but he is best known for his many short impressionistic piano solos, written first under the influence of Tchaikovsky but later turning aganist Romanticism as he experimented with the whole-tone scale.

AB 2345

A LITTLE SLOW WALTZ

(En lille langsom Vals)

NIELSEN, Op.11 No.3

Carl Nielsen (1865–1931) was the seventh of 12 children who grew up in humble circumstances in a Danish village. He learned the violin at an early age, joined a military band in his teens and, after studying at the Copenhagen Conservatory, played in the orchestra of the Royal Chapel. He later established himself in the musical life of the city as a conductor, teacher and composer. Best known for his orchestral works, he wrote a few piano pieces, this one coming from an album of *Humorous Bagatelles*.

AB 2345

AT THE SMITHY

(Chez le forgeron)

MAIKAPAR, Op.8 No.5

Samuil Maikapar (1867–1938) was born in the Ukraine. After graduating from law school, he attended the St Petersburg Conservatory and then studied the piano with Leschetizky in Vienna. From 1910 to 1930 he was professor for piano at the St Petersburg Conservatory. His compositions are almost entirely for the piano, the most successful being in miniature form and written for children. This piece comes from an album of *Novelettes mignonnes*.

Ped. come prima

STUDY in G

GEDIKE, Op.36 No.26

Of German descent, Alexander Gedike (1877–1957) was born in Moscow into a musical family. He studied under Arensky and Ladukhin at the Moscow Conservatory and was appointed professor of piano there at the age of 26, later teaching chamber music and the organ as well. He appeared in Russia and abroad as a concert pianist and was also a notable organist. He composed four operas, four concertos and three symphonies as well as much piano music.

STUDY in G minor

DUNHILL, Op.74 Bk II No.5

Thomas Dunhill (1877–1946) was born in London and studied composition under Stanford at the Royal College of Music, where he was to become a professor after teaching for ten years at Eton College. He first made his name as a composer of chamber music and later turned his attention to the orchestra with music for two ballets and some light operas. His educational output, particularly for the piano, was extensive, this study coming from his graded series *The Wheel of Progress*.

AB 2345

PRAYER

GLIÈRE, Op.43 No.2

Reinhold Glière (1875–1956) was born in Kiev and studied at the Moscow Conservatory, where he was later to become professor of composition, Khachaturian and Prokofiev being two of his many pupils. Besides appearing on the concert platform both as conductor and pianist, he composed a number of large-scale works, including seven ballet scores which mark him out as one of the founders of Soviet ballet. He also wrote for chamber groups, for the voice and for the piano. In this second of his *Eight Easy Pieces*, the pedalling is editorial.

MINIATURE PASTORAL No.2

BRIDGE

Frank Bridge (1879–1941) was born in Brighton and studied under Stanford at the Royal College of Music. He took an active part in the musical life of London, playing the violin and viola in chamber groups and conducting at the Promenade Concerts. His early compositions were mainly chamber music and songs, but later he wrote several orchestral works. He also taught composition, Britten being one of his pupils who did much to establish the composer's reputation after his death. In this piece, one of six pastorals written in 1917, the pedalling is editorial.

Copyright 1918 by Winthrop Rogers Ltd. Reprinted by permission of Boosey & Hawkes Music Publishers Ltd.

AB 2345

DONKEY RIDE

Allegretto con spirito [♩. = c.88]

SWINSTEAD

Felix Swinstead (1880–1959) was born in London and studied at the Royal Academy of Music, where later he was appointed professor of piano, a post he held for nearly 50 years. For a long time he was also an examiner for the Associated Board. His published works were numerous, mainly consisting of pieces for the piano, often written for educational purposes. This one comes from his album *The Young Idea*.

CLOWNS

KABALEVSKY, Op.39 No.20

Born in St Petersburg in 1904, Dmitri Kabalevsky was able to play the piano by ear at the age of six. After deciding against a career in mathematics, he studied composition at the Moscow Conservatory where later he was to teach. His output as a composer includes six operas, four symphonies, six concertos, chamber works, and scores for ballets and films, but he is probably best known for his piano music for young children.

THE LOST LAMB

ALWYN

William Alwyn (1905–1985) was born in Northampton. He studied the flute, piano and composition at the Royal Academy of Music and subsequently taught there from 1926 to 1955. His orchestral works include five symphonies and three concerti grossi, and he also wrote over 60 film scores, most notably those for *Odd Man Out* and *The Fallen Idol*. Among his other works are operas, chamber music, songs and a few piano pieces. This one comes from his suite *April Morn*.

AB 2345

Processed and printed by
Halstan & Co. Ltd., Amersham, Bucks., England